Words to stitch by

Express your creativity—and your sentiments—with these popular Cross Stitch designs by Lori Markovic. Whether you're looking for the right words to thank a friend, brighten a family member's day, or remind yourself and others that "nice matters," you can't go wrong with these pleasing patterns. Also included are traditional verses to decorate a nursery or declare your love. Why not treat yourself with a sampler that echoes the sweet simplicity of an earlier era? All eight designs are perfect to stitch for gifts, for your home, or just for fun!

Meet Lori Markovic

If you're just discovering the design work of Lori Markovic, you're in for a real treat! In each of her La-D-Da cross stitch pieces, Lori combines the homey appeal of primitive samplers with a touch of modern flair.

"I started cross-stitching when my children were little," says Lori. "Then, a little over a decade ago, some vintage sampler books caught my eye at the library. I wanted to try designing a sampler, because I was thinking a lot about the girls who stitched those Early American pieces. Their lives were all about family, home, and faith—ideals that run through all generations. And that's how I started La-D-Da Designs.

Lori and husband Bob live in Wisconsin, where they are happily surrounded by family. Lori likes to garden and bird watch, which no doubt inspires many of the natural elements in her designs. Another inspiration is the strong sense of community she enjoys with fellow cross-stitchers.

Lori says, "As a designer, I've had the opportunity to meet many stitchers across this country and am amazed by their generosity and kindness. Cross Stitch is truly a gentle art for gentle souls."

LEISURE ARTS, INC.
Maumelle, Arkansas

*T*hree perky flowers celebrate a happy union on this thoughtful wedding or anniversary present. Personalize it with the couple's initials, the date of the event, and your own initials so they will always enjoy your good wishes.

Chart is on pages 14 and 15.

$\mathcal{W}$hen a friendship lifts your spirits and adds more joy to your life, let that friend know how special he or she is to you!

Chart is on pages 16 and 17.

*B*ecause she brightens your days, you'll love stitching this whimsical verse for your daughter. And because you made it just for her, she'll treasure it forever.

Chart is on pages 26 and 27.

Remember these words from a popular children's song? It was composed in 1943, and the original lyrics were written as "Mairzy doats and dozy doats,"—just for fun!

Chart is on pages 12 and 13.

*N*ice does indeed count, yet on a challenging day that fact can be a tad difficult to recall. That's why it's helpful to have this pleasant reminder nearby. It's not only pretty; it's also a practical aid for everyday living!

Chart is on pages 20-23.

Sometimes, you just want to spend a little time making something lovely. This old-fashioned sampler was inspired by the practice pieces young girls used to stitch more than a century ago. It is simple, visually expressive, and delightful to have around.

Chart is on pages 10 and 11.

*T*he whimsy and innocence of a child's song becomes a sweet theme in this homespun-look Cross Stitch piece. What a perfect decoration for a nursery or playroom!

Chart is on pages 24 and 25.

*M*odern roses create a lush garland above a classic rhyme. It's a romantic design that mixes vintage charm with contemporary style.

Chart is on pages 18 and 19.

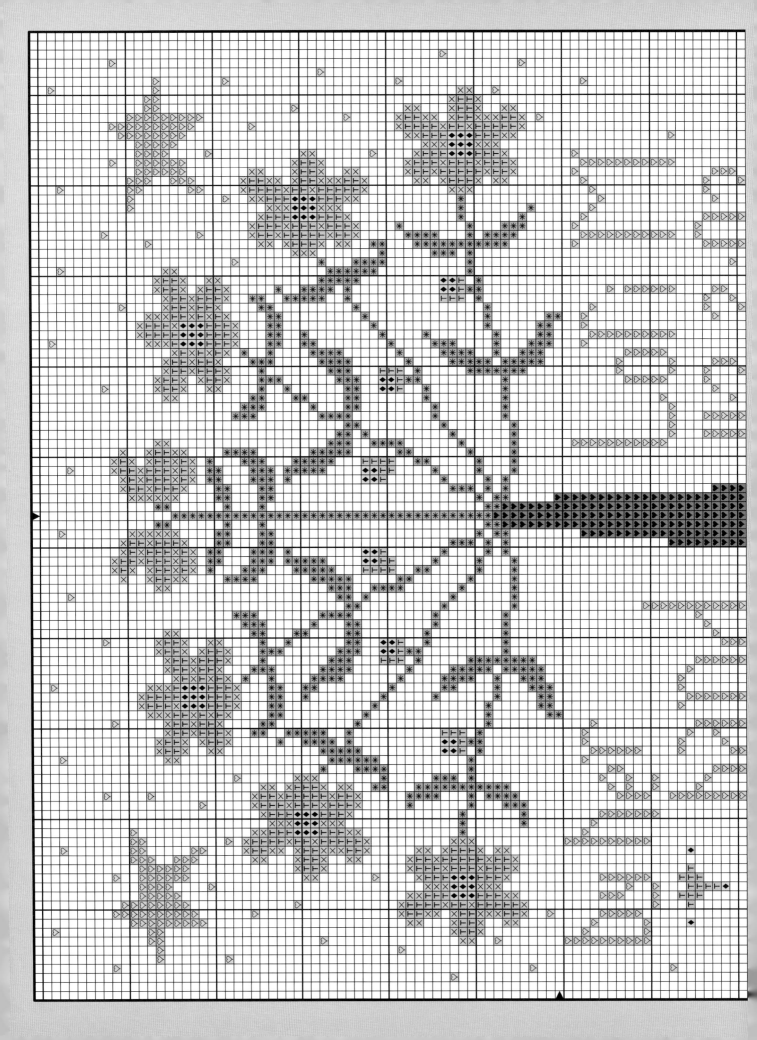

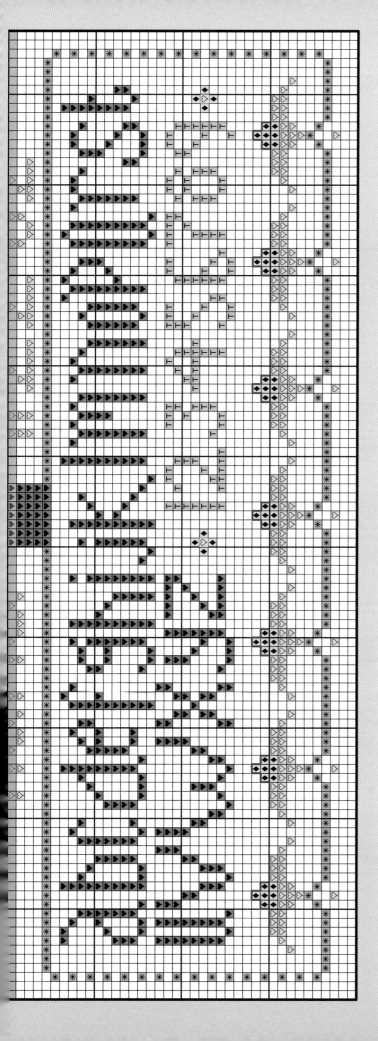

X		B'ST	DMC	SUL	COLOR
SAMPLER THREADS					
Nutmeg		◹	356	45079	terra-cotta
Cinnamon			433	45094	brown
Banker's Grey			646	45152	grey
Gold Leaf			729	45173	gold
Wood Smoke			840	45238	lt brown
Shutter Green			3363	45349	green
Indicates last row of top section.					

T	◤	▽	◆	✕	✳	▨

Stitch Count: (103w x 117h)

14 count	7³⁄₈" x 8³⁄₈"
16 count	6¹⁄₂" x 7³⁄₈"
18 count	5³⁄₄" x 6¹⁄₂"

By Her Hand

(shown on page 7) was stitched over
2 fabric threads on a 12" x 12½" piece of
hand-dyed linen (36 count). One strand
of Sampler Threads from The Gentle Art
was used for Cross Stitch and Backstitch.
Personalize the design by adding the
stitcher's name or initials and the date
stitched using the alphabets and numbers
on the chart and on page 28. The design
size is 5³⁄₄" x 6½". The design was
custom framed.

Mares Eat Oats

(shown on page 5) was stitched over 2 fabric threads on a 13½" x 11½" piece of hand-dyed linen (36 ct). One strand of Sampler Threads from The Gentle Art was used for Cross Stitch. The design size is 7⅜" x 5½". The design was custom framed.

X	SAMPLER THREADS	DMC	SUL	COLOR
♥	Mulberry	221	45044	red
■	Black Crow	310	45053	black
✕	Nutmeg	434	45095	brown
♡	Grecian Gold	832	45233	golden olive
T	Forest Glade	936	45278	green
	Indicates first row of right section.			

Stitch Count: (131w x 98h)

14 count	9⅜" x 7"
16 count	8¼" x 6⅛"
18 count	7⅜" x 5½"

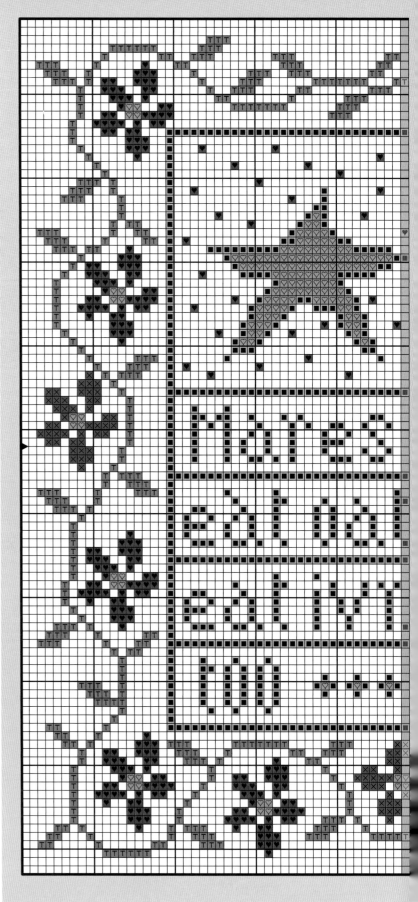

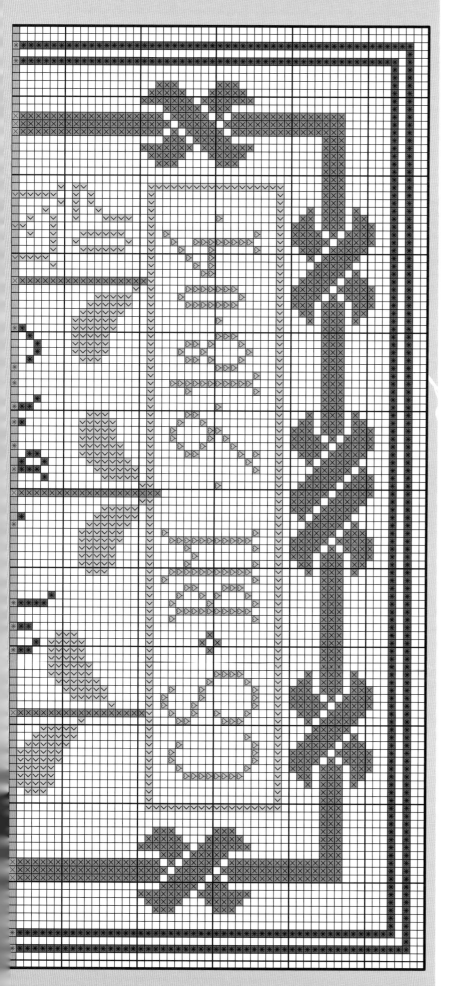

The Tie that Binds

(shown on page 2) was stitched over 2 fabric threads on a 12½" x 14½" piece of Cream Brulee Linen by R&R Reproductions (36 ct). One strand of Needlepoint, Inc. Silk was used for Cross Stitch. Personalize the design by adding the stitcher's initials and the year stitched, and the initials of the couple and their wedding date using the alphabet and numbers on page 28. The design size is 6½" x 8⅛". The design was custom framed.

X	NPI	DMC	SUL	COLOR
⟡	765	435	45096	gold
T	341	613	45146	tan
✕	315	830	45231	olive
∨	292	3052	45332	green
✳	967	3787	45395	grey
►	126	3857	45455	red brown
▨				Indicates last row of top section.

Stitch Count: (116w x 145h)

14 count	8⅜" x 10⅜"
16 count	7¼" x 9⅛"
18 count	6½" x 8⅛"

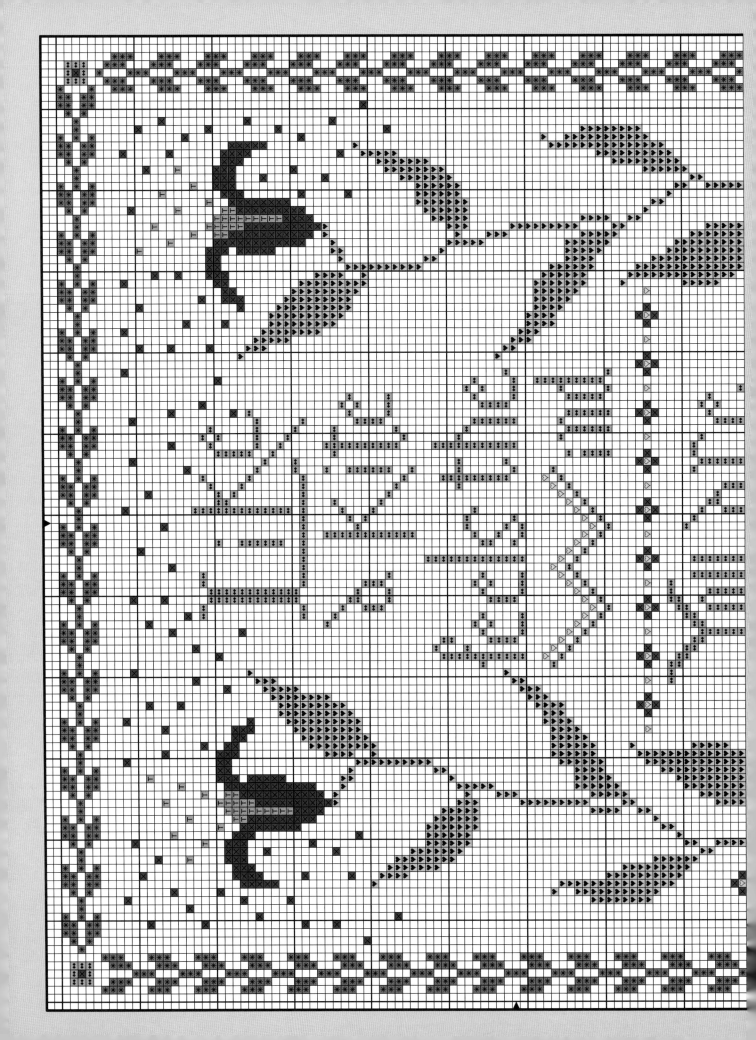

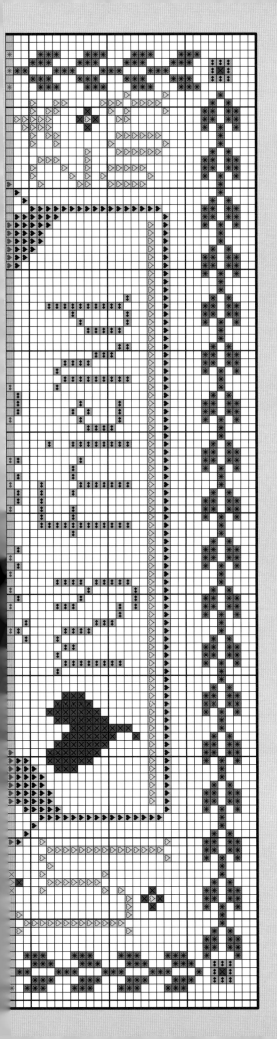

	SAMPLER THREADS	DMC	SUL	COLOR
X				
⬨	Banker's Grey	451	45101	grey
✳	Blue Spruce	500	45109	blue green
‡	Peacock	924	45269	blue
T	–	976	45305	gold
▶	Shutter Green	3051	45331	green
✕	Mulberry	3777	45390	red
▨	Indicates last row of top section.			

Stitch Count: (116w x 117h)

14 count	8³/₈" x 8³/₈"
16 count	7¹/₄" x 7³/₈"
18 count	6¹/₂" x 6¹/₂"

My Friend

(shown on page 3) was stitched over 2 fabric threads on a 12¹/₂" x 12¹/₂" piece of Mockingbird Linen by R&R Reproductions (36 ct). One strand of Sampler Threads from The Gentle Art (DMC 976 for gold) was used for Cross Stitch. Personalize the design by adding the stitcher's initials and the year stitched using the alphabet and numbers on page 28. The design size is 6¹/₂" x 6¹/₂". The design was custom framed.

17

Roses are Red

(shown on page 9) was stitched over 2 fabric threads on a 15¹⁄₂" x 11" piece of Kansas City Blend Linen by R&R Reproductions (35 ct). One strand of Sampler Threads from The Gentle Art was used for Cross Stitch. Personalize the design by adding the stitcher's initials and the year stitched using the alphabet and numbers on page 28. The design size is 9¹⁄₂" x 4⁷⁄₈". The design was custom framed.

X	SAMPLER THREADS	DMC	SUL	COLOR
✻	Old Hickory	610	45143	brown
T	Chamomile	3032	45324	tan
✕	Dried Thyme	3051	45331	green
♥*	Old Red Paint	3721	45365	red
▨	Indicates last row of left section.			

*Work Cross Stitches with Sampler Threads in a circular pattern to give depth to the roses.

Stitch Count: (165w x 85h)

14 count	11⁷/₈" x 6¹/₈"
16 count	10³/₈" x 5³/₈"
18 count	9¹/₄" x 4³/₄"

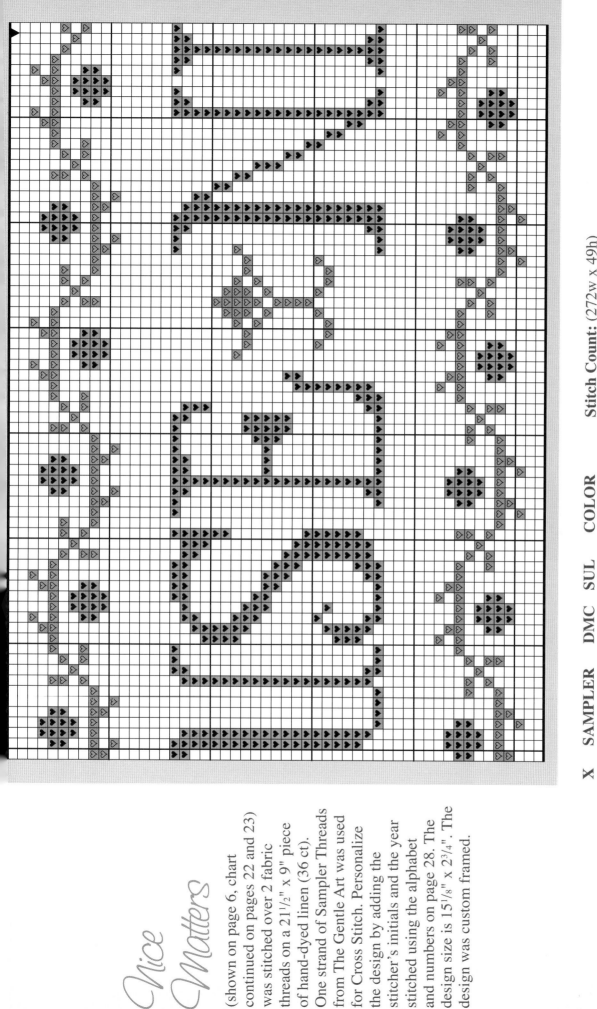

Stitch Count: (272w x 49h)

14 count	19¹/₂" x	3¹/₂"
16 count	17" x	3¹/₈"
18 count	15¹/₈" x	2³/₄"

X	SAMPLER THREADS	DMC	SUL	COLOR
⊠	Grecian Gold	834	45235	golden olive
▶	Soot	3799	45397	grey
▢	Indicates first or last row of adjacent section.			

(shown on page 6, chart continued on pages 22 and 23)

Nice Matters

was stitched over 2 fabric threads on a 21¹/₂" x 9" piece of hand-dyed linen (36 ct). One strand of Sampler Threads from The Gentle Art was used for Cross Stitch. Personalize the design by adding the stitcher's initials and the year stitched using the alphabet and numbers on page 28. The design size is 15¹/₈" x 2³/₄". The design was custom framed.

21

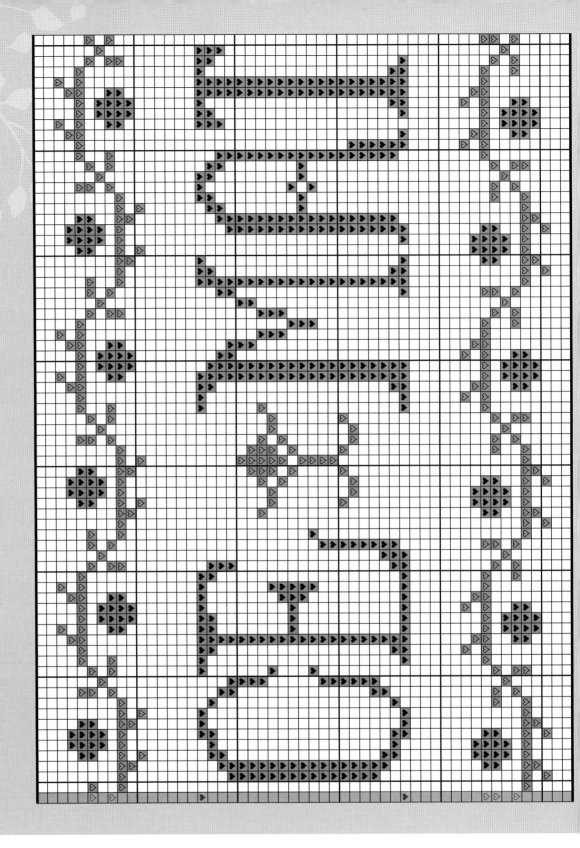

X	SAMPLER THREADS	DMC	SUL	COLOR
	Grecian Gold	834	45235	golden olive
	Soot	3799	45397	grey
	Indicates first or last row of adjacent section.			

Stitch Count: (272w x 49h)

14 count	19½"	x	3½"
16 count	17"	x	3⅛"
18 count	15⅛"	x	2¾"

Nice Matters

(Chart continued from pages 20 and 21.)

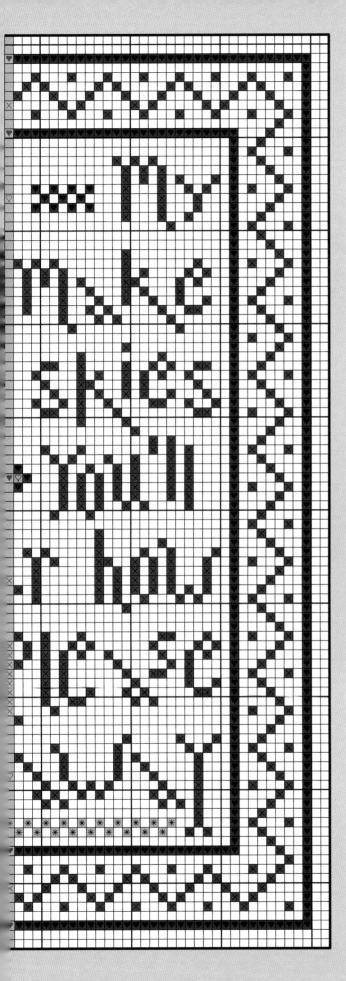

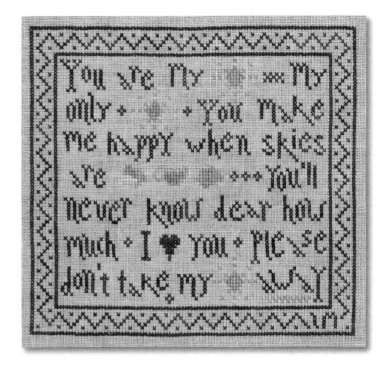

My Sunshine

(shown on page 8) was stitched over 2 fabric threads on a 12½" x 11½" piece of Kansas City Blend Linen by R&R Reproductions (35 ct). One strand of Crescent Colours cotton floss was used for Cross Stitch. If desired, personalize the design by adding the stitcher's initials in the bottom right corner. The design size is 6¼" x 5⅜". The design was custom framed.

X	CRESCENT COLOURS	DMC	SUL	COLOR
✳	River Rocks	451	45101	grey
♡	Old Oak Tree	832	45233	golden olive
▼	Manor Red	902	45252	burgundy
✕	Black Coffee	3371	45351	brown black
▦	Indicates last row of left section.			

Stitch Count: (109w x 94h)

14 count	7⅞" x 6¾"
16 count	6⅞" x 5⅞"
18 count	6⅛" x 5¼"

Merry Sunshine

(shown on page 4) was stitched over 2 fabric threads on a 14" x 13" piece of hand-dyed linen (35 ct). One strand of Needlepoint, Inc. Silk was used for Cross Stitch. Personalize the design by adding the stitcher's initials and the year stitched using the alphabet and numbers on page 28. The design size is 7³/₄" x 6⁵/₈". The design was custom framed.

X	NPI	DMC	SUL	COLOR
✳	313	832	45233	golden olive
T	976	3021	45428	grey
✕	933	3740	45371	purple
◇	122	3772	45386	rose brown
♥	903	3829	45426	gold
▢	Indicates first row of right section.			

Stitch Count: (135w x 114h)

14 count	9³/₄" x 8¹/₄"
16 count	8¹/₂" x 7¹/₈"
18 count	7¹/₂" x 6³/₈"

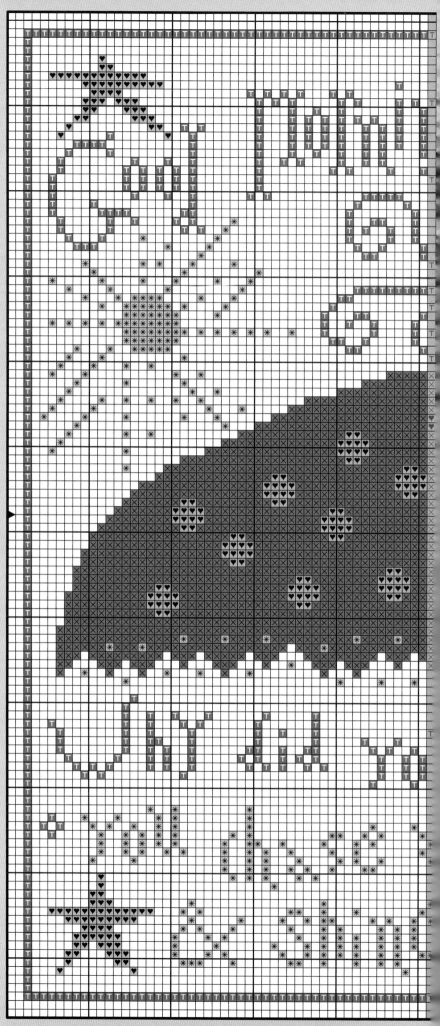

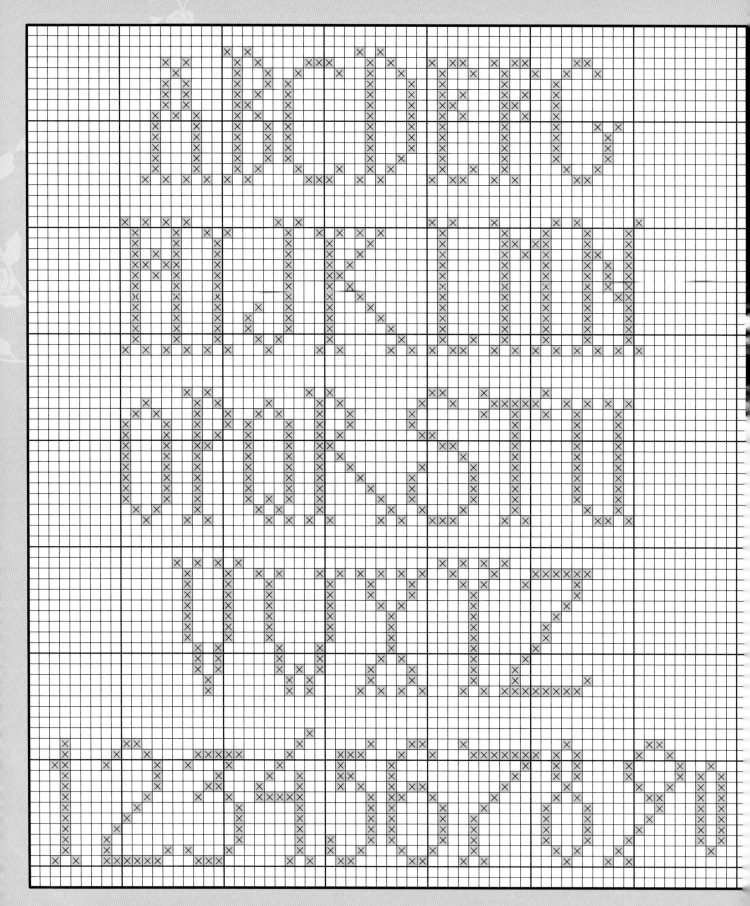

Designer Tip:
Lori altered her initials and dates, "nesting" and offsetting the letters and numbers for a unique design. Use this alphabet as is or change it as you like.

General Instructions

USING HAND-DYED FLOSSES AND FABRICS

Hand-dyed flosses and linens have variations, sometimes very subtle, in shading. In order to maintain these variations, it is safer to not wash your hand-dyed items, before or after stitching. Wash your hands before each stitching session and store your project in a clean location.

DETERMINING THE SIZE TO CUT YOUR FABRIC

1. The stitch count, width and height, is provided for each project. The design size is also listed for certain fabric thread counts. To determine the design size for fabric thread counts not listed, follow Steps 2 and 3.
2. Divide the width number by the thread count of your fabric. This gives you the width of your design in inches when stitched on that particular count fabric.

Examples

63 squares wide ÷ 14 count Aida = $4^1/_2$" wide
63 squares wide ÷ 18 count Aida = $3^1/_2$" wide
63 squares wide ÷ 28 count linen over 2 threads = $4^1/_2$" wide

3. Repeat the process to determine the height of the design.
4. When cutting the fabric, add at least 3" to each side of the design.

WORKING WITH FLOSS

If using more than one strand of floss, separate strands and realign them before threading your needle to ensure smoother stitches. Keep stitching tension consistent. Begin and end floss by running it under several stitches on the back; never tie knots.

HOW TO READ CHARTS

Each chart is made up of a key and a gridded design where each square represents a stitch. The symbols in the key tell which floss color to use for each stitch in the chart. The floss type used in the photo model is listed in the key first, then other flosses which may be used instead are listed with their conversion numbers or names. Use the same number of strands indicated regardless of the type of floss you choose. Be aware that using a different floss will give your stitched piece a different appearance. The following headings and symbols may be included:

X – Cross Stitch
B'ST – Backstitch
DMC – DMC color number
SUL – Sullivans color number
SAMPLER THREADS – Sampler Threads or Simply Shaker Sampler Threads from The Gentle Art color name
CRESCENT COLOURS – Crescent Colours color name
NPI – Needlepoint, Inc. Silk color number
COLOR – The name given to the floss color in this chart

A square filled with a color and a symbol should be worked as a Cross Stitch.

A straight line should be worked as a Backstitch.

HOW TO STITCH

Always work Cross Stitches first and then add the Backstitch.

Cross Stitch (X): If using hand dyed floss (The Gentle Art Sampler Threads, Weeks Dye Works floss, or Crescent Colours floss), work one complete Cross Stitch at a time before moving to the next Cross Stitch (**Fig. 1**). When working over 2 fabric threads, work Cross Stitch as shown in **Fig 2**.

Fig. 1

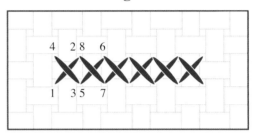

Fig. 2

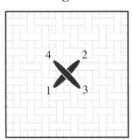

If using DMC, Sullivans, or silk floss, work as follows: For horizontal rows, work stitches in two journeys (**Fig. 3**). For vertical rows, complete each stitch as shown (**Fig. 4**). When working over 2 fabric threads, work Cross Stitch as shown in **Fig. 5**.

Fig. 3

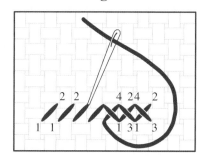

Fig. 4

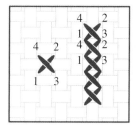

Fig. 5

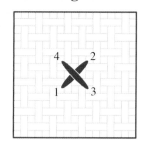

Backstitch (**B'ST**): For outlines and details, Backstitch should be worked after the design has been completed (**Fig. 6**). When working over 2 fabric threads, work Backstitch as shown in **Fig 7**.

Fig. 6

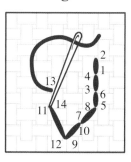

Fig. 7

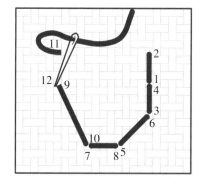

WORKING OVER TWO FABRIC THREADS

Use the sewing method instead of the stab method when working over two fabric threads. Keep your stitching hand on the right side of the fabric and take the needle down and up with one stroke. To add support to stitches, it is important that the first Cross Stitch is place on the fabric with stitch 1–2 beginning and ending where a vertical fabric thread crosses over a horizontal fabric thread (**Fig. 8**). When the first stitch is in the correct position, the entire design will be placed properly, with vertical fabric threads supporting each stitch.

Fig. 8

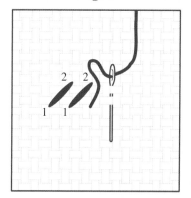

FINDING YOUR SUPPLIES

Fabrics and floss may be found at Cross Stitch shops and limited assortments of items may be found at craft stores. If a shop is not available to you, there are several Cross Stitch shops online. Also, information may be found online at these sites.

Hand-dyed floss: www.thegentleart.com,
     www.weeksdyeworks.com, and
     www.crescentcolours.com
Silk floss: www.needlepointsilk.com
Cotton floss: www.dmc-usa.com and
     www.sullivans.net/usa/sullivansfloss
R&R Reproductions Linens: www.dyeing2stitch.com

Production Team

Writer: Frances Huddleston
Editorial Writer: Susan McManus Johnson
Senior Graphic Artist: Lora Puls
Graphic Artists: Becca Snider and Janie Marie Wright
Photographer: Ken West
Photography Stylist: Sondra Daniel

We have made every effort to ensure that these instructions are accurate and complete. We cannot, however, be responsible for human error, typographical mistakes, or variations in individual work.